JOHN DEERE

What's New on the Farm?

PARACHUTE PRESS

LONDON, NEW YORK, MUNICH, MELBOURNE, and DELHI

First Edition, 2009

Published in the United States by DK Publishing
375 Hudson Street, New York, New York 10014

09 10 11 12 13 10 9 8 7 6 5 4 3 2

Created and produced by Parachute Publishing, L.L.C.
322 Eighth Avenue, New York, NY 10001

Written by Catherine Nichols
Designed by Alisa Komsky

ISBN 978-0-7566-4446-8

Printed in China
November 2009, second printing

Discover more at
www.dk.com

The publisher would like to thank the following for their kind permission to reproduce their photographs.

ABBREVIATIONS KEY: t-top, b-bottom, r-right, l-left, c-center, a-above, f-far, bkgd-background, bo-border

Cover images
Front Simone van den Berg/Shutterstock.com (tl); Pakhnyushcha/Shutterstock.com (tr); Juliya W. Shumskaya/Shutterstock.com (bl)
Back Digital Vision/Punchstock.com (tl, tr)
Half-title Eric Isselée/Shutterstock.com (c)
Title page Eric Isselée/Shutterstock.com (tr); Digital Vision/Punchstock.com (tl); Digital Vision/Punchstock.com (cr); Chiyacat/Shutterstock.com (cl)
4-5 SNEHIT/Shutterstock.com (4)
6-7 Photodisc/Punchstock.com (6); saied shahin kiya/Shutterstock.com (7tl, 7tr, 7bl); Lana Langlois/Shutterstock.com (7br)
8-9 Kileman/Dreamstime.com (8); Eric Isselée/Shutterstock.com (9tl, 9tr); Wikus Otto/Shutterstock.com (9bl); Pakhnyushcha/Shutterstock.com (9br)
10-11 Corbis/Punchstock.com (10tl); Digital Vision/Punchstock.com (10tr); slattery613/iStockphoto.com (10b); Westend61/Punchstock.com (11)
12-13 Stocktrek/Corbis (12bkgd); Linda Bucklin/Shutterstock.com (12bfl); Alan Carey/Corbis (12bll); Amanda Flagg/Shutterstock.com (12br); Costin Cojocaru/Shutterstock.com (13bll); Mark Winfrey/Shutterstock.com (13br); Drimi/Shutterstock.com (13bfr)
14-15 Juliya W. Shumskaya/Shutterstock.com (14bl); Matthew Jacques/Shutterstock.com (14c); Digital Vision/Punchstock.com (15tr)
16-17 fotohunter/Shutterstock.com (16br); Jenny Horne/Shutterstock.com (16bl); Christopher Walker/Shutterstock.com (16cl); Kevin M. Kerfoot/Shutterstock.com (17)
18-19 Patrick Power/Shutterstock.com (18tl); Anne Kitzman/Shutterstock.com (18r); Shutterstock.com (18l); EugeneF/Shutterstock.com (19t)
20-21 ulga/Shutterstock.com (20); hans.slegers/Shutterstock.com (21tr); ansem/Shutterstock.com (21tl); Thinkstock/Punchstock.com (21b)
22-23 Shutterstock.com (22t); Yuliya Kutishchev/Shutterstock.com (22b); Eric Gevaert/Shutterstock.com (23)
24 Noam Armonn/Shutterstock.com (cl); Gallo Images ROOTS RF/Punchstock.com (tl); Cultura/Punchstock.com (bl); Kevin M. Kerfoot/Shutterstock.com (tr); Arvind Balaraman/Shutterstock.com (br)
Stickers Digital Vision/Punchstock.com (t, c); Eric Isselée/Shutterstock.com (r, ctl); Fotocrisis/Shutterstock.com (cbl); Chiyacat/Shutterstock.com (b)

All other images © Deere & Company.

Every effort has been made to trace the copyright holders of photographs, and we apologize if any omissions have been made.

JOHN DEERE

What's New
on the Farm?

PARACHUTE PRESS

Life on the Farm

What's new on the farm?
Let's take a look around and find out.

These tractors are turning over the soil, cutting grass, and spraying crops.

Look and See

Tractors are busy on the farm. They work all over the land.

The Chicken Coop

Our first stop is the chicken coop.
Hens lay lots of eggs here.

Look and See

Chickens eat grains, seeds, and even insects. They peck at the food with their sharp beaks.

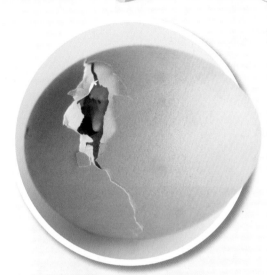

Baby chicks grow inside the eggs.

In about three weeks, the chicks are ready to come out, or hatch.

A chick is so small, it can fit in the palm of your hand.

How many chicks have hatched so far?

By the Pond

Look at all the geese and ducks
that live by the pond.

A baby goose is called a gosling.

A baby duck is called a duckling.

A duckling's webbed feet help it to paddle in the water.

Look and See

When these fuzzy yellow ducklings are all grown, they will have white feathers just like their mother.

Pigs in a Pen

Guess who's new at the pigpen?
Lots and lots of baby pigs!

How many babies did this
mother pig have?

A baby pig is
called a piglet.

Look and See

On hot days, pigs like
to roll around in the
mud to cool off.

These piglets are getting ready for a nap!

Barnyard Babies

Some brand-new babies are in the barnyard.

A baby horse
is called a foal.

A baby goat
is called a kid.

A baby sheep
is called a lamb.

Look and See

Some barnyard babies eat hay. This machine makes hay into huge round bales.

A baby llama is called a cria.

A baby donkey is called a foal.

A baby rabbit is called a kit.

In the Pasture

The pasture is where cows graze, or eat grass.

Cows eat hay, too.

Look and See

This tractor is pulling a machine that mixes hay and feed for the cows to eat.

A baby cow is called a calf.

The Pumpkin Patch

All around the farm, seeds are being planted. Many crops will grow from the tiny seeds.

Look and See

Tractors pull planters that drop seeds into the soil.

Pumpkins start out as seeds.

The seeds grow into tiny plants called seedlings.

The seedlings grow into big plants.

Look at all the pumpkins in the pumpkin patch!

In the Cornfield

Corn plants grow in fields.

This seedling
is a corn plant.

Watch it grow taller and taller.

This delicious corn is almost ready to eat!

Look and See

After the combine harvests the crop, the corn is used to feed farm animals.

The Apple Orchard

Let's visit the apple orchard. Each spring, new flowers cover the branches of the trees.

New flowers are called blossoms.

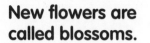

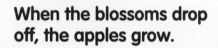

When the blossoms drop off, the apples grow.

Look and See

This tractor helps carry apples to a farmers' market.

The Meadow

Many sheep are in the meadow. They nibble on the green grass that grows there.

Like all babies, lambs need lots of sleep.

Look and See

A sheep's coat keeps it warm. One day these lambs will have thick wool just like their mother.

The Growing Farm

So much happens on a farm.
What new things would you like to do?

Pet a foal.

Pick apples in an orchard.

Feed the animals.

Go on a hay ride.